Efficient
BOOK WRITING

A Strategic Program for Improving Writing Productivity

Kasthurirangan Gopalakrishnan, Ph.D.

Transdependenz LLC

CONTENTS

Dedicated to my

Teachers

With utmost gratitude!

INTRODUCTION

"A writer is someone for whom writing is more difficult than it is for other people."

- Thomas Mann

❊

Do you find it hard to start on your writing project? Or is it that you struggle to finish what you started? Sometimes you write for few days and then abandon it for months together for whatever reason. Sometimes you just have no clue of what you want to write about. You can't get started until you know everything about what you want to write. I have experienced all these (and many more that are hard to list) unclear phases in my writing journey and still experience them sometimes.

In my opinion, the reason we are unable to consistently and steadily produce as much as we want to, apart from other realistic constraints, is that we do not take a systematic and strategic approach to our writing projects. Yes, some don't need any kind of a writing system. They may be able to produce a best-seller overnight. Exceptions are exceptions. But, for most of us who are interested in developing good writing habits leading to consistent and steady levels of writing productivity, having a strategic writing system is a must.

The reason is very simple. Writing is both an art and a science. The science of writing includes some standard and fundamental Do's and Don'ts that are repeatable. When applied, they lead to reproducible results with some margin of error. For instance, try writing something creative or insightful after taking a very heavy meal. Almost always, you are going to feel drowsy and give up on your writing. I say almost always because you may be able to make an exception to this rule sometimes under certain very favorable conditions. Of course, the opposite is not necessarily true. It is not that you will start filling page after page if you write with an empty stomach.

Writing is certainly an art because it takes deliberate practice to become an effective writer. As much as simply reading about or even hearing music is not actually going to make you a seasoned musician, unless you apply yourself to the writing practice with persistence, it is very difficult to achieve steady levels of writing output. Persistence is the key because you should not become influenced by the short-term failures and successes that come from your daily application to the art of writing.

Having a writing system that includes a writing plan after realistically examining your writing situation, some sort of an outline, and a toolbox of simple tips and habits to overcome barriers to writing and streamline your writing routine will help you to start and complete your writing project with the least amount of stress and frustration.

I am not talking about a universal writing system that is set in stone, but a personalized and flexible writing system customized to the evolving needs of every writer. And that which incorporates the lessons learned along the way as you get comfortable and better at it.

Efficient Book Writing presents a systematic and strategic approach to book writing that includes proven time prioritization strategies, productive writing techniques, and effective anti-procrastination habits. In that sense, I have not tried to create a new approach to writing, but simply compiled and synthesized the existing information in a manner that is hopefully engaging and easier for you, the reader, to assimilate and benefit. Hopefully, the ideas and strategies presented here will motivate you to develop your own writing system that you can apply to any of your writing projects.

This introductory-level book is divided into five parts that together form a strategic program for achieving steady levels of writing productivity, whether you are writing an article, essay, blog, or book. As one should have a writing plan before starting to build content, Part I focuses on this aspect by asking you to identify your purpose behind writing a book, consider your target audience, and examine your writing situation. Part II teaches you how to gather ideas for your book writing project and create your outline which will serve as the initial roadmap for your book. In Part III, you learn how to develop your book's content and go from the first draft to the final draft. Part IV helps you to systematize your writing process by addressing various barriers to writing, including perfectionism and negative self-talk, and discusses some simple solutions to go after inspiration, rather than "wait for the muse". Part IV is special to me. I have noticed that many of us regularly avoid writing by keeping ourselves busy with low-priority tasks. This is at the heart of writing procrastination. Therefore, this last part helps you to get your writing done by introducing some practical strategies and tips for overcoming procrastination and developing healthy writing habits.

Although I often present examples and ideas in the context of writing a book, the techniques discussed here are adaptable to any of your writing projects.

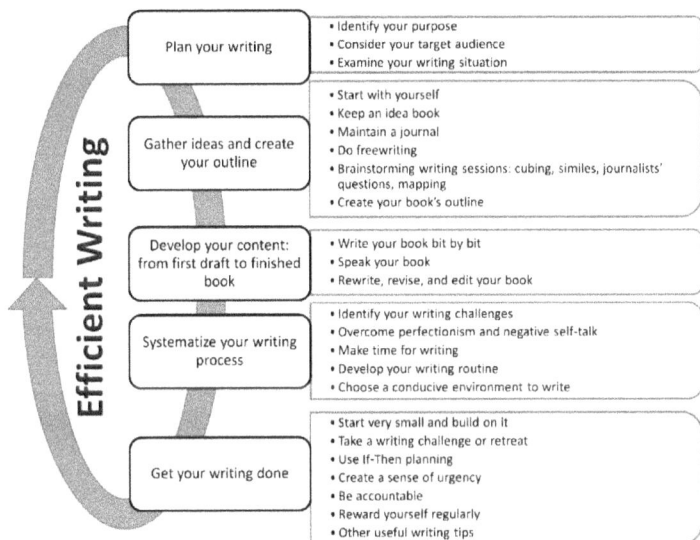

⌘

PART I: Plan Your Writing

⌘

IDENTIFY YOUR PURPOSE

"Why do I write? Persons have an inner urge to make sense of their worlds and to communicate that sense-making to others. As part of the human situation I can give and receive, care and be cared for, stimulate and be stimulated. I write in order to share my searchings, to show I care, and to stimulate and be stimulated. I feel best about writing when I have ideas to which I must give birth."

- Louise M. Berman

❀

When you are driven by a purpose that is meaningful to you, you are far more likely to accomplish something than when you don't have one. According to recent research, what drives people at work is not money, but a meaningful purpose they are able to connect to their jobs – that they are able to make a difference or offer some kind of benefit or value to others through their work.

So, what is your purpose behind writing a book? If you are not clear about your purpose, then ask yourself, "Why am I doing this? What will happen if I don't write this book? What do I expect from writing this book? How will it impact my personal and professional life? What impact does it have on my self-esteem?"

Writing is a long-haul process and although you may start off the project with great enthusiasm and energy, what will really help you to not run out of steam is to have a grounded purpose and to keep revisiting this purpose again and again.

Are you writing to establish yourself as an authority on the topic you are writing about? May be you have discovered a fantastic way to get something done more efficiently and want to see the rest of the world benefit from it just as you have benefitted? It need not be any of these, but something as simple as self-development or wanting to learn a subject or topic more thoroughly. Often times, you learn much better about a subject when you teach it to others.

You may be writing to just communicate ideas and thoughts. You may be writing just for enjoyment. Are you impelled from within to write such that nothing can stop you? For some people, it is the professional recognition that can be achieved through writing. And for academics, it could very well be rewards through tenure, promotion, salary increments and so on.

Some of us may be writing to feel more complete. When we say we want to communicate our ideas and thoughts, it is not just with others. It is with ourselves for shaping our thoughts and redefining our purposes in life.

Your purpose may not be fully clear in the beginning, but may become clearer as you go along in your writing. In other words, as you read through this book, you'll begin to understand how you can use the process of writing itself to connect with yourself deeper. Sometimes, when you start writing about a particular subject, you learn so much about it that it makes a big impact on your life itself.

Whatever purpose you are able to identify now, it is very important to write it down on a piece of paper and possibly read it at least three times a day: once before you start to write, once after you have completed your writing session for the day, and once before you retire for the day. You may want to write the entire purpose or a keyword associated with it on a sticky note and paste it on your desk to constantly derive inspiration from it as you go through the highs-and-lows of writing.

At the level of content, 'What is the purpose of your book?' takes a different meaning. Remember when you have to write an academic essay for your college assignment, they talked about two broad purposes: *informative* and *persuasive*. The same thing applies to book writing as well. Do you want to inform the reader of the latest developments in a specific field or the benefits of developing a certain habit? Or Do you want to present strong arguments to persuade the reader to think differently of a certain topic? Often times, an engaging book will seamlessly integrate both these purposes.

APPLICATION EXERCISES

1. Why do you want to write a book?

    _____

    _____

    _____

    _____

2. What will happen if you don't write this book?

_____

_____

_____

_____

3. How will the writing of this book impact your personal and professional life?

_____

_____

_____

_____

4. What impact does writing of this book have on your self-esteem?

_____

_____

_____

_____

WHO IS YOUR AUDIENCE

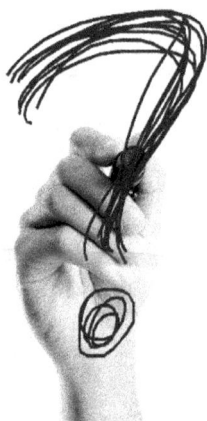

CONSIDER YOUR TARGET AUDIENCE

"Forget your generalized audience. In the first place, the nameless, the faceless audience will scare you to death. And in the second place, unlike the theatre, it doesn't exist. In writing, your audience is one single reader. I have found that sometimes it helps to pick out one person – a real person you know, or an imagined person – and to write to that one."

- John Steinbeck

❦

Now that your writing is driven by a purpose, it is time to consider your target audience. Your potential readers. You do have a message for your readers that you would like to communicate. But, 'how to communicate' is as important as or even more important than 'what to communicate'. Professional writers know this well as they always write to delight their target audience.

As George Gopen and Judith Swan wrote in their popular American Scientist article, The Science of Scientific Writing, *"If the reader is to grasp what the writer means, the writer must understand what the reader needs."*

Here is a very simple example, but makes the point. Let us say you want to write a book on how to improve one's reading comprehension and speed. It becomes immediately clear that your approach to writing will be quite different depending on whether you are writing this book for early readers or students at college or entrepreneurs and so on.

What differentiates engaging and impactful writing from monotonous writing is whether or not the writer has kept the potential reader in mind while writing. Many times, we forget that we are actually writing to someone.

Keeping your audience in mind while writing your book has several benefits:

- It helps you to more easily decide what materials to include and what not to include in your writing.

- It helps you to decide on your writing style. Of course, the latest trend, especially in e-book publishing, is that you write in a conversational tone, as if you are speaking to a friend sitting across the table, and not in an overly technical language with the need to look up every fifth word for meaning. This helps the reader to get to the heart of your content right away and also has a wider appeal.

- It helps you to decide on how much to explain (i.e., can you see the forest for the trees?) and match your choice of words and tone to match your reader's expectations.

- It helps you to organize your ideas and consider different approaches to writing and how to best present your for-and-against arguments.

APPLICATION EXERCISES

1. Who is your target audience?

_____

_____

_____

_____

2. If you think you have more than one category of audience, list all of them here.

_____

_____

_____

_____

3. What does your audience want from you? What do they value?

_____

_____

_____

_____

4. What is most important to your audience? Why should your book matter to them?

_____

_____

_____

_____

Examine Your Writing Situation

"We are not worried by real problems so much as by our imagined anxieties about real problems."

- Epictetus

Even before you start researching your topic or draft an outline for your book, it is important to have a writing plan that includes realistic evaluation of your writing situation.

A writing plan helps you to plan for any expected or unexpected obstacles on the way and helps you to achieve steady levels of productivity. With a writing plan, you are able to better track your progress and adjust for any extenuating circumstances. You understand that you don't have to finish your writing project in one or two days, but break into smaller tasks and sub-tasks and continually make progress on it day by day.

How much time can you put in every day towards your book writing project? As we will see in later chapters, cultivating a daily habit of writing is the best way to achieve sustained and steady levels of productivity and progress. If you find that you have a lot of unstructured time, some time management strategies discussed later in this book may be helpful to sharpen your book writing focus.

Are you going through a career change, family expansion, or vacation? Are you going through some stressful situations at work or at home? Whatever it is that may impact your writing time and effort, put that into the plan. The more complex your life is, the more detailed your writing plan needs to be.

I totally understand that those of us living with children and/or elders needing special care will find it very difficult to make time for writing. This is the time to plan for it. It is admittedly difficult to plan for it unless you have the support of your friends and family members.

As you examine your writing situation, this is also the time to address your initial anxieties or fears about writing. After deeply considering your audience, are you feeling nervous about your writing because you have never written to such an audience before? After finding out that your target readers have been overly critical of other books in your category/niche, are you afraid that your work also come under severe criticism? May be memories of growing up in an excessively critical environment are preventing you from taking up this book writing project?

If we don't examine our writing anxieties or fears and seek appropriate remedies, they can turn into resistances and present themselves as excuses to sabotage our writing progress later on. Often times, when we say we don't feel like writing, the hidden excuse is that we have some kind of fear about the outcome. More to come on this in a later chapter when we actually get into the process of writing. Right now, we are just examining the initial anxieties that may surface as we start planning to write a book.

It is important to recognize that most of these anxieties and fears you may be experiencing are situational and not long-standing or pervasive in your writing life. Some key strategies for handling these feelings, also commonly referred to as "writers' block" are presented in my book, *The Productive Academic Writer*. Here is a simple summary:

- Choose a writing partner or a writing buddy from whom you can get support, encouragement and feedback.

- Did you know that you don't have to actually "write" to get a book written? You may find yourself more comfortable speaking your book or portions of your book and then transcribing it to get your first draft. Given the recent explosion and success of conversational-format nonfiction books, there is no reason not to try out this method. More on this later.

- Remember that there is only so much a writer can say on a topic at a given point in time and in a given situation. You can't cover every single detail related to your particular topic as there is always more to be said on any given topic. If you do find that your chosen topic is too broad or has multiple audiences, you may consider bringing them out in the form of a series of short books. For instance, instead of writing a single monumental piece on "time management", you may consider writing a series of short books on time management: time management for students, time management for entrepreneurs, etc.

- Cultivate a habit of rewarding yourself with simple successes in your writing life such as getting started, drafting the outline, etc. Keeping a log of these positive writing experiences and writing successes can give you the strength and confidence to face complex writing challenges later in your life.

APPLICATION EXERCISES

1. How much time can you put in every day towards your book writing project?

_____

_____

_____

_____

2. What challenges and obstacles do you foresee in starting and completing your book?

_____

_____

_____

3. What are some of your anxieties and fears about writing this book?

_____

_____

_____

⌘

PART II: Gather Ideas and Create Your Outline

⌘

START WITH YOURSELF

"The aim of art is to represent not the outward appearance of things, but their inward significance."

- Aristotle

❋

We'll assume that you already have some idea of what you want to write about. If not, some ideas presented in the following chapters may stimulate you to identify your book topic.

First, start with yourself as the source before even looking up what others have written on that particular topic. Before directly plunging into researching about your topic or doing a literature review, draw on your own experiences and your prior knowledge of that topic.

At the outset, it does feel like you have nothing to write. It may very well be a topic that you discuss day in and day out with your friends and co-workers. It could be a topic that is of great interest to you. Still, when it comes to writing a book on that topic, it feels like a heavy burden crushing you under its weight. But, actually that's not true.

In the next few chapters, we'll be looking at some of the ways to gather ideas for writing your first book. These are proven strategies to uncover what you already know about the topic.

As we go through these various strategies for gathering ideas for your writing, you'll discover with surprise that you know much more about the topic that you want to write a book about than what you think. These different tips will uncover what you already know about the topic and bring them out on paper in a natural way. They will provide leads and even the draft outline for your book from which point your book writing journey is going to be a lot easier and manageable.

As we go through these various idea gathering paradigms, it is important to remember that not all of them may work in all writing situations. Similarly, what works for one individual may not work for another. That is why we are going to discuss different approaches to it such that you can pick and choose what suits your situation better. But, I do encourage you to try all the methods even if you have found out the one that works the best for you.

Always remember that as long as you keep mulling over ideas and topics in your mind, you are always in muddy waters. Clarity comes when you start putting pen to the paper or your hands to the keyboard. Through the process of writing, your thoughts translate into concrete ideas. Writing is thinking. And the more organized you can get to be before starting to actually write your book, the better it is.

So, here are some of the well-known prewriting techniques which will be discussed in the next few chapters in greater detail: keep an idea book, maintain a journal, freewriting, and brainstorming.

Keep an Idea Book

"Be less curious about people and more curious about ideas."

- Marie Curie

To live your life means to be open to ideas and experiences around you and to be intellectually and emotionally curious. Good writers are always curious and continually developing themselves, learning the world around them. So, always carry with you an idea book or flash cards to jot down what you see, what you experience. Ideas can come anytime and can also vanish like snowflakes anytime. They can pop up when you take your shower or when you speak to a friend or while you go on a walk.

An idea book is especially useful if you are already contemplating one or more book topics. I don't know if you have observed this. When you take special interest in something, you start noticing things related to your object of interest in greater detail that previously went unnoticed.

For instance, when I took interest in buying a good car, I suddenly found myself noticing the make, model, and all other details right about every car that I saw on the street. They were there previously too. But, it was when I took interest in buying a good car and wanted to know all about cars, that my eyes and ears were open to actively seeking information about every car that I came across. Psychologists refer to this as "selective perception". Once your mind has focused on some object, you will start noticing its presence or absence everywhere.

Similarly, the idea behind keeping an 'idea book' is that great ideas can come to you anytime, especially about the topic you are thinking to write about. So, you keep yourself open to them by always carrying a pocket-sized notebook and a pen, or alternatively a Smartphone, to capture them on the go. Creative directors and copywriters refer to this idea book as a 'swipe file' – a growing collection of ideas that can serve as a useful reference for new ideas and projects.

The actual process of note-taking is more important than the tool you choose to use. The advantage of carrying a digital idea book is that it is always on the go and you could also include audio and video clips in note-taking. There are many multi-platform apps available for such notes-taking on the go such as Evernote and oneNote.

APPLICATION EXERCISES

1. Review the entries in your idea book over the past week and see if you find anything interesting there that you can write about.

    _____

    _____

    _____

    _____

    _____

2. Do you carry a physical (pen-and-notebook) or digital idea book or both? Are you equally comfortable with both or do you prefer one over the other?

    _____

    _____

    _____

    _____

    _____

3. Identify one book topic that interests you. Let few days pass by. How useful was your idea book in recording ideas and thoughts relevant to that topic (hint: selective perception)?

MAINTAIN A JOURNAL

"Learn from yesterday, live for today, hope for tomorrow. The important thing is to not stop questioning."

- Albert Einstein

❋

Many writers, experienced as well as amateur, also maintain a journal. Unlike a diary where you record your daily events, a journal is a place where you capture the inner movements of your thoughts and emotions in response to one or more specific situations. It is a place to have a conversation with yourself, letting go of all worries about the correctness of your thoughts and feelings. There is no censoring involved. It is not like a peer-reviewed or even a self-reviewed journal, but a record of random thoughts and records. It is introspective and self-reflective.

Your journal is your personal space for developing ideas and thoughts as you interact with the world around you. Amazingly, many times you'll find that in that free flow of thoughts, you'll find hidden gems which are new ideas for your writing projects or a conflict resolution for your fiction and so on. This is because you have been thinking about the problem in your mind. But you didn't allow the solution to come to you freely because of thinking about it too much somewhat rigidly. But, it is when you allow yourself to 'brain-dump' freely, the solution comes to you freely.

Some fiction authors recommend the use of a 'sense diary' where you record emotions. You take one experience in a day and write about it. For instance, take the meal you had at lunch and fully describe the emotions and sensations associated with that experience. Again, this forms a good writing habit and broadens your thinking about writing.

Journaling helps you to build the habit of daily writing. The more you write, the more you get into the mindset of a writer. You'll always find that when you start writing, your focus and concentration improves because writing requires concentration. Even 15 minutes of such journaling every day can make a huge difference in overcoming your inner fears about writing and give you the confidence to move forward. Even if there is no time to write, you can speak into your mobile device and later transcribe it into your journal, if you have that time.

Journaling also helps you to develop the habit of close observation and critical thinking. It can also serve as an excellent resource when you are looking for ideas or topics to write about. For instance, Lynn Quitman Troyka, the author of *Handbook for Writers*, gives the example of a college student who received an assignment to write an essay on how to face an extraordinary challenge. As she was reading through her journal for ideas to narrow down her essay topic and scope, she found a journal entry on what it was like facing a real tornado in Wichita, Kansas. This inspired her to choose that (how to face natural disasters) as her essay topic.

APPLICATION EXERCISES

If you are new to journaling or have been out of touch for some time, here are some ideas and journaling prompts to get going.

1. Write down 3 good things that happened to you today that you feel grateful for, small or big. Try to do this for a week.

   _____

   _____

   _____

   _____

2. What is your idea of a "perfect day"?

   _____

   _____

_____

_____

3. Take a classic novel that you like and write a short
   description of what it may look like if it were to be
   written for kids, academics, entrepreneurs, etc.

_____

_____

_____

_____

Do Freewriting

"Forget all the rules. Forget about being published. Write for yourself and celebrate writing."

- *Melinda Haynes*

❧

Freewriting is basically a great way to get your writing gears moving. It helps you to break free from the "blank screen" syndrome (the dangerous syndrome of staring at the blank screen for a long time - that plagues most beginning writers) and gives you the satisfaction of filling page after page without having to critically evaluate it. A form of freewriting that is well known in literary circles is stream-of-consciousness writing.

When it comes to writing a book, you can either do one or more initial freewriting sessions on the topic you have already identified or if you don't have topic yet, you can use freewriting to stimulate your thinking process (i.e., do a "brain-dump"). The emphasis here is on speed over everything else. Freewriting is especially effective when you set a goal like "write for 10 minutes" or "write 500 words or 2 pages". Most of what you produce through freewriting, especially at this stage, may appear to be of no use, but you'll also come across some gems of ideas.

After doing the initial freewriting to gather some momentum in writing, you want to keep the ball rolling by doing a focused freewriting on a specific topic or idea. Either choose a topic or idea related to your central topic and do a freewriting on it. Similar to freewriting, keep going until you reach your writing goal or until the timer stops. Don't censor anything, but let your thoughts flow into paper naturally.

One simple way to prevent yourself from reviewing or criticizing what you have written is to dim your PC or laptop monitor or turn it off so that you can't read what you are writing until the end of the session. It is always good to use a timer before you engage in a freewriting session.

If you don't know what this freewriting is all about, here is an excellent advice offered by Peter Elbow, *Writing Without Teachers*:

> *Don't stop for anything. Go quickly without rushing. Never stop to look back, to cross something out, to wonder how to spell something,*

to wonder what word or thought to use, or to think about what you are doing. If you can't think of a word or a spelling, just use a squiggle or else write "I can't think what to say, I can't think what to say" as many times as you want; or repeat the last word you wrote over and over again; or anything else. The only requirement is that you never stop.

Here is an excerpt from focused freewriting on the phrase "worrying":

Why do we humans always worry? What makes us worry? It appears that everyone worries about something or other. The rich worry, the poor worry. The educated worry, the uneducated worry. The haves worry, the have-nots worry. Everyone worries. But, are we meant to worry or are we meant to be free of worries? If worrying is our natural state, then surely there wouldn't be so many books written on how to overcome worries and how not to worry. There wouldn't be so many TV shows and podcasts trying to cheer us up and make us forget about all the worries at least temporarily.

APPLICATION EXERCISES

1. Try freewriting for 5 minutes without stopping just about anything that comes to your mind.

   _____

   _____

   _____

   _____

   _____

   _____

2. Try focused freewriting on the following phrases/topics: standing in a queue at the bank; lessons learned from an ant; what is in it for me?

   _____

   _____

   _____

   _____

   _____

   _____

3. What was your experience during and after freewriting? Do you perceive more clarity or confusion after freewriting? Do you find any new

ideas or inspirations in your freewriting about your book?

_____

_____

_____

_____

_____

_____

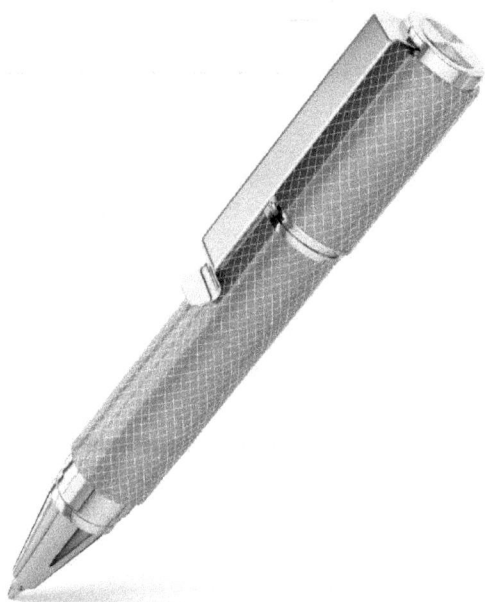

HOLD BRAINSTORMING WRITING SESSIONS

*"No problem can be solved from the same level
of consciousness that created it."*

- Albert Einstein

❋

Brainstorming is a process to generate as many ideas as
possible relating to a specific topic or interest. It
maximizes the ability to generate ideas by suspending
judgment and by separating the idea creation process and
the evaluation process. The idea behind brainstorming
seems to have come from Alex Faickney Osborn (1888-
1996) who used the term brainstorming in his work, *Your
Creative Power*, published in 1948. According to Osborn, a
"brainstorm" means "using the brain to storm a creative

problem and do so in commando fashion, with each stormer attacking the same objective."

In a brainstorming writing session, you formulate your writing topic in the form of a problem and jot down all the ideas you can come up with in the form of a list. They can be words, phrases, or even random sentences, however wild they may appear to be. Here the focus is on quantity and not on evaluating the ideas, similar to a freewriting session. While originally meant to be a group activity, brainstorming can be equally or even more effective when done by oneself because there is no fear of criticism leading to the generation of a wider range of ideas.

A brainstorming session can be conducted on a specific idea related to your main topic or the main topic itself if you are not sure what it should cover. It can also be used to generate arguments for and against a topic you are interested in.

While brainstorming, if you feel that you are running out of ideas, here are some ways suggested by *The Writing Center* at the University of North Carolina at Chapel Hill that you can use to stimulate your thinking.

CUBING

Cubing is a way to consider your topic from six different perspectives just as a cube has six different faces. In this technique, you take a sheet of paper, consider your topic and jot down your responses to the following six requests:

- Describe it
- Compare it
- Associate it
- Analyze it
- Apply it
- Argue for and against it

When you look at your responses, do you see any pattern that can naturally lead to grouping of topics and sub-topics? Do you see any new ideas emerging? If not anything else, this should help you to create a broader awareness of the topic you are writing your book about.

SIMILES

The use of similes can also facilitate brainstorming. In this technique, you take a sheet of paper and write the following sentence:

_____ is/was/are/were   like
_____

Now, on the left side of the blank, write a term or concept that your book focusses on. Fill in the right blank with as many answers that you can come up with and jot them all down. After you have completed this exercise, you can look over your list to see if any new ideas came up and whether you can use any portions of this in your book or in outlining your book.

Use Journalists' Questions

> *"I keep six honest serving-men (They taught me all I knew);*
>
> *Their names are What and Why and When And How and Where and Who."*
>
> *- Rudyard Kipling*

Journalists often use the following six questions to get a complete picture of a story:

- Who
- What
- When
- Why
- Where
- How

This is also referred to as the Five Ws or the Five Ws-and-One H. These are exploratory questions that force you to approach a topic from multiple perspectives. Let us say you want to write a book on how to survive an earthquake:

- Who: Who are at higher risk of injury or loss when an earthquake strikes? Whom to approach for help in the event of an earthquake? Who does research on studying and publishing about earthquakes? Who needs earthquake insurance?

- What: What causes an earthquake? What are its various causes? What is the difference between minor and major earthquakes? What to do when an earthquake occurs? What does it mean to survive an earthquake? What are the various survival supplies one needs to stock? What happens if you are not prepared? What lessons can you learn from other disaster survival experiences?

- When: A timeline of major earthquakes? Does it typically happen during daytime or nighttime?

- Why: Why has the number of earthquakes increased dramatically over the past few years? Why do people knowingly live in earthquake-prone areas? Why is it important to be prepared for an earthquake?

- Where: Where do earthquakes typically occur? Do you live in an area prone to quakes? Do earthquakes occur near the surface or deep below the surface? Where can you find more information about surviving an earthquake?

- How: How can you help your neighbors or friends after an earthquake? How to locate your nearest fire and police stations? How to organize your disaster supply kit? How to find about the seismic safety of your home? How to minimize the chances of injury or loss of property?

Now, take a topic that is of interest to you and write down the answers to these six questions: who, what, when, why, where, and how.

MAP YOUR IDEAS

Mapping is especially great for visual learners or visual thinkers. In this technique, you take a sheet of paper (or combine two sheets to make one large sheet) or use a blackboard/whiteboard. There are two primary ways to go about mapping.

Method 1

In the first method, you write down the central topic in the middle of the sheet and draw a circle around it. Now, write down major subdivisions of the topic around the central topic and connect each one of them to the central topic. Continue the same process for each of the major subdivisions by writing further subdivisions around them.

Method 2

In this method, you write the central topic in the middle of the sheet with a word or a short phrase. Jot down all ideas and thoughts related to the central topic on the left, right, top, bottom – slowly filling the whole sheet without censoring any of those thoughts associated with the central topic. You can always take out any idea that doesn't belong here at the end.

After you can't find any more ideas to write down, you start making clusters and relationships by circling terms that are related to each other and connecting them with lines. Continue this process until you can associate and connect as many terms as possible with each other. To differentiate between different concepts and terms, you could use different colored lines, lines with varying thicknesses, etc.

What you'll see in the end is a mind-map of your whole book – a spider web like figure. This is a great way to get the outline for your book.

Here is an initial map that I came up with when I was searching for ideas to write about "The Art of Listening" or "The Art of Speaking Less and Hearing More".

Finally, you need to incubate your ideas to grow them and develop them further. Especially, when you are trying to solve a problem in writing, like when your ideas are too thin or you have too much to write about and you want to shorten them.

There are different ways to incubate. One is to fully concentrate on a specific thought and let the mind relax and wander back to the writing problem. Another way is to not focus on any specific thought but let the mind wander from one thought to another and let it wander back naturally to the writing problem. You may see some light that you didn't see before.

APPLICATION EXERCISES

1. Which among the various brainstorming techniques discussed in this chapter do you find useful and why?

_____

_____

_____

_____

_____

_____

2. Prepare a list of journalists' questions on the following book topics: sustainable gardening; how to learn a new language?; critical thinking.

_____

_____

_____

_____

_____

_____

_____

_____

CREATE YOUR OUTLINE

Once you have made a plan for writing and organized yourself in terms of how much time you need to complete your book and where to find it on a daily basis, you'll find that your writing is going to be faster and better. And all the resources at your disposal are going to synergistically work in favor of you rather than against you. This is because you have a reasonably clear idea of where you are heading and what obstacles and challenges to expect. That is also the reason why you should have an outline for your book before you start to write.

After completing one or more of brainstorming writing sessions, you will have either a list of keywords or phrases or even better a map, from which you can develop your book outline.

Having some kind of an outline, even a rough one, is like having driving directions when you want to get from place A to place B. Irrespective of whatever it is that you are writing about, an outline helps you to keep up the writing momentum and not get stuck in the middle of your writing and feel frustrated.

Once you have an outline, it is much easier to focus on one sub-section at a time and start building your writing project. Until you have an outline, it is all in in your mind and it is very difficult to hold all the ideas there.

Typically, the core of a book outline will consist of Introduction followed by Chapter 1, Chapter 2, etc. Try to keep your outline flexible (and it is meant to be that way) such that the order of chapters can be switched around later, if needed.

How to outline your book? You may use a pen-and-paper or a Word processing software or Trello or Scrivener to develop your outline. Irrespective of what you choose to use, the basic process is similar. Based on the outcome of your brainstorming writing sessions, you record the main headings and sub-headings and bulleted list of points that you like to talk about under each heading/sub-heading.

Once you have an initial outline, it is time to develop your book's content and get the first draft completed. Broadly speaking, there are two primary ways you can get it accomplished. In the first approach, you actually write the book in small chunks by considering each topic/sub-topic. In the second approach, you actually speak the book by interviewing yourself or having someone interview you with a set of questions on each of your book's topic. In the next section, we'll primarily discuss these two approaches in more detail.

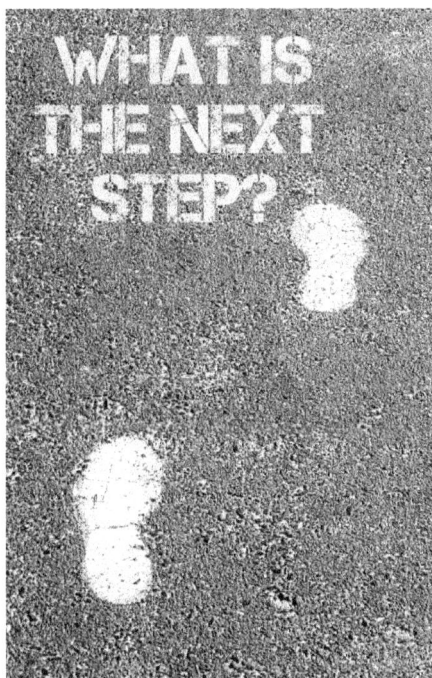

⌘

PART III: Develop Your Content:

From First Draft to Finished Book

⌘

WRITE YOUR BOOK BIT BY BIT

"The process of writing is a process of learning; and much has become clearer to me in the attempt to transform my original rough notes into what I hope is an intelligent presentation."

- Paul A. Baran

Now that you have an outline, you know the major topics and sub-topics that will be covered in your book. Take one specific topic at a time and focus on building content. You could do this through one or more scheduled writing sessions devoted to each topic. The key is to take one topic at a time and dive deep into to it to unearth information that is of interest to your readers.

You may find it helpful to write down each topic on a separate index card and reflect on it during the day as and when you get time. Note down any inspiration, idea, keyword, or phrase that may come to you (go back to your idea book) so that you can expand on it during your scheduled writing session.

If you are finding it hard to get started, use one or more brainstorming writing sessions (which you are already familiar with) on each of your book's topic to identify things that should be covered. Especially, use the journalist questions (Who, What, When, Why, Where, How) to think from your reader's perspective and to raise relevant questions and answer them.

Here are some questions that you may raise to probe into each of your topics further (these are some standard questions that apply to most informative book topics):

- What it is and what it is not?

- Why is it important or relevant in today's world?

- Who are the experts or those who have successfully mastered it?

- How to do it? Is there one particular way to do it? Or Are there several different ways to do it?

- What are the constraints?

- What are the economic aspects?

- What are the safety aspects?

As you do research and/or review published and unpublished sources to gather information to assist in your writing, use these questions as lenses to look for information that you need. Otherwise, the whole process of researching and reviewing literature can be overwhelming and exceedingly time consuming with very little output. If I take the stance that I will not begin to write until I have read every single piece of information that is available on my topic, I'll never be able to get started.

If you are unable to move forward with one topic after a certain point, move to another topic. You don't have to write linearly and sequentially if that is not working out for you. You can always reorganize your topics and make connections between different chapters later.

Employ the same freewriting technique that we previously discussed to get your messy first draft and save editing for the future drafts. As Henriette Anne Klauser, the author of *Writing on Both Sides of The Brain: Breakthrough Techniques for People Who Write* notes, "the work habit that underlies virtually all writing problems is the tendency to write and edit simultaneously". In other words, we should let go of the urge to edit as we write.

If you feel severely blocked, this is how you can use the five-minute freewriting technique to your advantage. Make a determination that all you need to do is to show up at the scheduled time to write for five minutes. In the beginning, even if you don't feel like writing, simply show up at the scheduled time, sit in your chair and start writing.

Use the freewriting advice offered by Peter Elbow to keep writing for five minutes, no matter what. Reward yourself at the end of your five-minute scheduled writing session. Once you feel familiar and comfortable with the five-minute freewriting technique, you will be able to gradually increasing your writing stints to longer durations.

The strategies presented in the next two sections, *Part IV: Systematize Your Writing Process* and *Part V: Get Your Writing Done*, will help you to identify your writing challenges, develop and streamline your writing process and master anti-procrastination writing habits. But, before we get there, I want to discuss how you can actually get your book written by speaking it if you are more comfortable with that approach rather than writing it.

Speak Your Book

"Writing is an intimate transaction between two people, conducted on paper, and it will go well to the extent that it retains its humanity."

- William Zinsser, On Writing Well

If you find it more comfortable to speak about one or more topics in your book than to sit down and write it, then use it to your advantage. Even 'writers' can use this method for variety or when they find it impossible to make progress with their writing.

In essence, this method helps you to first create your audiobook or portions of it and then transcribe it to get the content for your digital or print version. Here is a high-level summary of how you can put this method into action:

- Take one topic at a time from your developed outline

- Take the position of your reader and raise relevant and detailed questions (use the journalists' questions to stimulate your thinking)

- Consider the arguments you readers may raise with each of your answers and develop additional questions

- Either interview yourself or request your friend or writing partner to interview you and record the whole conversation

- Either transcribe the conversation yourself or have someone else transcribe it for you by paying some money (there are advantages to both)

This method is especially useful if you have a lot to say about your topic, but don't know where to start. You may be able to express yourself more freely without interruption through the medium of speech than writing. One of the biggest benefits of this approach is that you are actually letting your book speak to your reader, which is what a good book is supposed to do.

Now, let us imagine that you have to actually present your book to your reader(s) without putting them to sleep. What will go into your presentation slides or notes? How much to convey and how will you convey to keep them engaged? If you are unable to raise meaningful questions on your book's topic, try preparing a presentation on it. It is possible that you make frequent presentations surrounding your book's topic or have delivered speeches or short courses on similar topics.

Then, all you need is to get the audio/video recording of your talk transcribed and clean it up to produce the first draft.

I know that this method works because I recently employed it to 'write' an 8,000-word informative article in a very short time. I prepared a presentation on it and recorded myself delivering it. Then, I transcribed the audio recording as fast as I could. With some minor edits, the article was more or less ready to go.

Of course, I knew the topic well and I also knew what I wanted to say. But, still I was amazed at the result because it took me much less time to 'write' this article than it would have taken to actually write the article. Over and above everything, I was surprised that the article read more like a meaningful conversation which was the desired outcome. The topic was quite technical and my perfectionistic propensities would have made it very difficult to achieve this desired result.

One big advantage to transcribing the audio yourself is that you get to hear yourself speak about your book. This is reassuring. Also, the fact that you are able to type sentence after sentence at a high speed gives you a sense of accomplishment and the needed confidence to finish what you started. Another advantage is that it brings a heightened sense of focus that may inspire you to consider additional perspectives not covered in your talk. Of course, in the interest of time, you may prefer to get your audio recording transcribed by a third party like rev.com or transcribeme.com by paying some money.

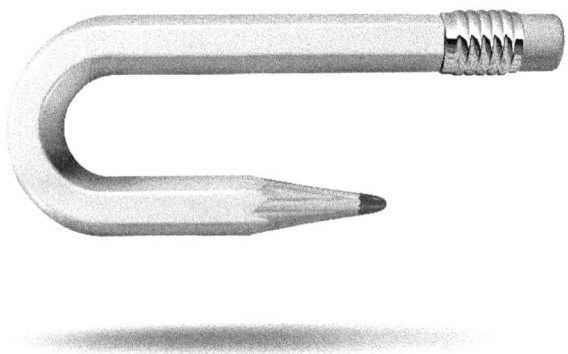

Rewrite, Revise, and Edit Your Book

"There is no great writing, only great rewriting."

- Justice Brandeis

Irrespective of whether you write your book bit by bit (previous chapter) or speak your book (this chapter), what you have in your hand is only a first draft, and not the final draft. You still need to flesh it out and revise it by getting a fresh pair of eyes on what you have written or imagining yourself as the reader looking at it for the first time.

One good strategy for revising and rewriting is to read out loud what you have written either by reading yourself, have your writing partner read it to you, or use a text-to-speech software application. It really helps you to catch any abrupt transitions, awkward sentences, gaps in explanations, etc. Finally, you also need to get your work edited to weed out unwanted phrases, fix awkward grammar, and ensure consistency and flow.

The process of rewriting, revising and editing to go from your first draft to final draft doesn't have to be long-drawn-out. The Writing Center at the University of North Carolina at Chapel Hill provides some very good advice on getting this task accomplished efficiently (http://writingcenter.unc.edu/handouts/revising-drafts/).

- Since we are very likely to become attached to our own writing (one reason is that the defense mechanism to prevent any criticism of our writing is at work), it is always a good practice to wait for at least few hours after you complete the initial draft before entering the revision and editing phase with an objective, unbiased lens.

- In the stage of rewriting and revising, don't focus on fixing your commas and periods, but try to focus on the big picture issues such as the overall flow, consistency, etc.

- See if you are maintaining focus on your original objective throughout your book or are you going off-tangent often? It is okay to stray off the topic sometimes just to break the monotony, but not at the cost of losing focus. Sometimes, at the end of completing your initial drafts, you realize that your topic has become too broad and that you have covered far more than what you had originally planned. If that happens, this is the time to consider if you want to break it into smaller book projects.

- After looking at what you have produced, do you feel that you have not really said anything new and that anyone else writing a book on the same topic would have said the same? Even if that's true, it's not a valid reason for giving up on your book project. Even if the idea or method that you are writing about is not new, you have expressed it in your own words in a new way which may help someone understand it better. Take courage from the words of Mark Twain: "There is no such thing as a new idea. It is impossible. We simply take a lot of old ideas and put them into a sort of mental kaleidoscope. We give them a turn and they make new and curious combinations."

- How balanced is your book? Do you greatly expand on few major topics and say very little about other topics? There is nothing wrong in that except that you need to make it clear to your readers the reason for doing so.

- Would your book read better by moving around topics/chapters? Are there real-life examples and applications you can include to add value to your discussions? Is the language appropriate for your target audience?

- To speed up your initial self-editing process, don't try to focus on grammar, style, consistency, formatting, etc. all at once. Rather, focus on one aspect of editing during every run-through. For instance, focus on just catching and fixing the misspelled words during the first revision, ensuring source attributions, verb tense consistency during the second revision, etc.

- Since we have a tendency to keep rewriting, revising and editing forever, the best way to get it done is to allocate a predetermined time limit and stick to it.

- As you develop content for your book, employ the simple and practical strategies outlined in the next two sections of this book to develop healthy writing habits, streamline your writing routine, overcome procrastination tendencies, and speed up your writing process.

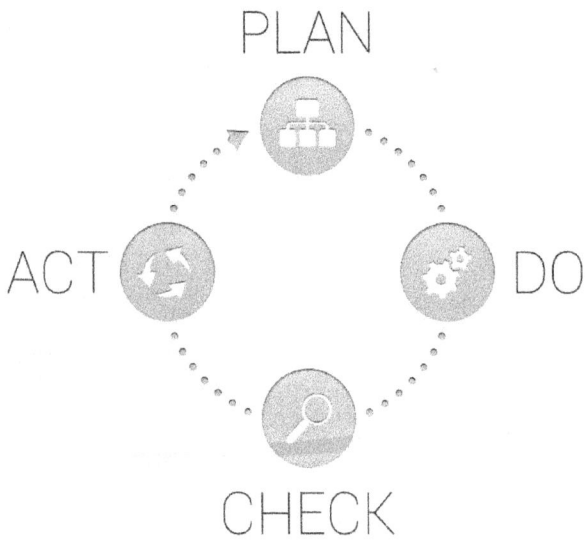

PLAN

ACT

DO

CHECK

⌘

PART IV: Systematize Your Writing Process

⌘

IDENTIFY YOUR WRITING CHALLENGES

"It's not the writing part that is hard. What's hard is sitting down to write. What keeps us from sitting down is resistance."

- Steven Pressfield

I want you to take two minutes and identify what are your biggest challenges to writing. It could be one thing or a number of challenges. They could be related to lack of resources, feeling of boredom, or feeling of being overwhelmed. Obviously, the more specific you can get with respect to identifying what your challenges are, the better it is.

For instance, "I just don't feel inspired to write" can often be the excuse for not writing. But, it is not very specific and doesn't give you clues on how to address it. It is true that inspiration is real, especially in the field of creative arts, where much of what is produced is based on inspiration. But, the problem is to hold inspiration as an excuse for not making the effort. It could become a negative habit where one feels that one is not able to write because one doesn't feel like writing. We want to replace this negative habit with another positive habit of writing whether we feel inspired or not.

Are you able to pinpoint your writing challenge(s)? As they say, half the river is crossed simply by knowing what the problem is.

External challenges are those that are beyond our control. It has to do with, for instance, the people we work with or the people who exert certain influence over us professionally, emotionally, etc. These are the challenges that we can't do much about. So, we want to focus on internal challenges because we can do something about them.

Internal challenges manifest in the form of resistance to writing in subtle, clever ways.

For instance, you determine yourself to write and you are all set to write. But, then suddenly you are overtaken by the urge to do something else and you end up doing that instead of writing. You keep yourself busy with something else other than writing and in this way you have managed to avoid writing which is what you had intended to do in the first place. It is a specific form of procrastination where you put off writing by keeping yourself busy with low-priority tasks.

We can deceive ourselves by saying that we need to do more research or do more analysis and give that as a convenient excuse to keep postponing our writing.

APPLICATION EXERCISES

1. Take two minutes to identify what throws you off right at that moment you start to write.

   _____

   _____

   _____

   _____

   _____

2. In your opinion, what are some of the major writing avoidance behaviors that you indulge in (ex., reading news articles, searching the internet without any goal or plan)?

   _____

   _____

   _____

   _____

   _____

   _____

   _____

3. What are some of your external challenges to writing, if any? Do you have a plan to work around them to keep up with your writing practice?

_____

_____

_____

_____

_____

_____

OVERCOME PERFECTIONISM AND NEGATIVE SELF-TALK

"Almost all good writing begins with terrible first efforts. You need to start somewhere."

- Anne Lamott

When we say we don't feel like writing, oftentimes the hidden excuse is that we have some kind of fear about the outcome. Sometimes the fears are rational, but many times, they are irrational. For instance, an academic writer may have the fear of being criticized when writing about a controversial research topic. The peer review process of evaluating academic writing is quite rigorous. It is meant to be that way because academic writing is often about contributing to the existing knowledge on a subject and there is intense scrutiny to ensure originality, accuracy, and correctness of what is being reported. That's a rational fear.

But, the fear of failure is irrational when its origin is in some form of 'perfectionism'. When we set a very high standard for what our writing should come out to be, we are setting ourselves up for frustration and failure because there is not a single piece of work that has been agreed upon by everyone. Not to expect to receive any criticism for our writing is an irrational fear. Rather, constructive criticisms serve to improve our writing more and more.

The biggest challenge to our productivity is to get that first draft out. Once we have the first draft in whatever shape, we have something to work on further and eventually churn out the final draft after a lot of revisions. But, without that first version, however disorganized and shabby it may appear, we have made zero progress in writing.

The perfectionist mindset is one major obstacle that often comes in the way of writing the first draft. Apart from the fact that what may be considered perfect writing is subject to debate and interpretation, the perfectionist approach towards writing sets up a very high expectation from ourselves right at the outset. All our mental energy and confidence can become drained in trying to meet those lofty expectations every time we set out to write with very little left to do the actual writing. This leads to a feeling of discouragement and eventual abandonment of our writing project. In summary, the perfectionist mindset doesn't lead to a healthy writing habit.

We need to understand that the healthy pursuit of excellence is helpful and energizing while the striving for artificial standards of perfection is unhealthy and disempowering.

Download the FREE overleaf from this website that lists some examples of common types of perfectionism behaviors: http://bit.ly/1WhYntq. You can use this as a checklist to observe if you are doing any of the activities mentioned in the list because of setting unrelenting high standards for yourself.

Here are some practical tips on how we can dismantle the striving-for-artificial-perfection mindset and accept a realistic striving-for-excellence mindset in writing:

- Don't think of your writing as the next earth-shattering masterpiece. Rather, consider it as a "rough first draft", "write-up", etc. and refer to it as such. Whether or not it will end up being a ground-breaking work is not something we can determine and is immaterial at the time of writing.

- Accept that "to err is human" and that we all make mistakes. No matter how hard we may try, we will still make mistakes. The best part of valor is to learn from our mistakes and not be afraid of making mistakes. This includes learning to make quick decisions on trivial issues (Which font to choose? What design template should I use to get the best results?), instead of not giving into the 'analysis paralysis'.

- Set your productivity goals (can even be a simple commitment as writing five minutes a day) after realistically taking into your consideration other priorities and commitments. Don't try to exponentially increase your writing productivity overnight thinking that your colleague was able to do so.

- Don't judge your output by how great you felt or how bad you felt while writing. In other words, don't judge your output at all. Be satisfied with the effort that you put into writing rather than being preoccupied with some kind of grandiose result that you think is going to come out of it. If you have met your productivity goal for the day, rejoice and congratulate yourself. If not, just wait for tomorrow's turn to try harder.

- By all means, seek social and professional support, feedback and guidance. To seek outside support is not a negative sign of weakness, but a positive sign of courage and a healthy desire to overcome your limiting beliefs that hinder your progress.

Another major obstacle to free-flowing writing is the defeatist mindset that can range anywhere from indulging in negative self-talk with our mind and with others who espouse a similar approach to developing a deep aversion to writing by repeatedly labeling ourselves with negative adjectives. Many writers refer to this self-defeating mindset as the "inner critic" or "inner bully" or the "the voice of the oppressor" which is generally associated with some fear of not being able to meet the goals or live up to one's standards.

Generally, the inner critic's voice is milder in the beginning, but grows louder and louder when you unconsciously struggle to ignore it or when you try to participate in a conversation with it. Instead of doing either, take few deep breaths to regain your awareness when your inner critic strikes and note down the first comment it makes on a piece of paper with full consciousness. The inner critic feels indeed gratified that you gave it due importance and eventually quiets down. Take another deep breath and carry on with your writing task.

The breathing exercise and mindful writing slows down your thoughts and puts you in a better position to silence your inner critic. Admittedly, this takes practice, but that is what productive writing is all about!.

APPLICATION EXERCISES

1. Write down one useful lesson you learnt from this chapter.

   _____

   _____

_____

_____

_____

2. Which of the following perfectionism behaviors
    do you see in yourself when it comes to writing
    (could be one or more): (a) overthinking of what
    should be the first sentence of your work and not
    being able to decide; (b) not wanting to write until
    you stock up all the resourceful items you need as
    a writer; (c) repeatedly giving up after writing a few
    sentences because you just don't feel good about
    what you wrote; (d) wanting to do everything by
    yourself for fear that no one else may be able to do
    things as good as you do.

_____

_____

_____

_____

_____

_____

3. Do you identify any patterns in your "inner critic"
    before, during, or after writing? Write down one
    solution that you plan to practice for replacing
    negative thoughts with positive, hope-giving
    thoughts.

_____

_____

_____

_____

_____

_____

MAKE TIME FOR WRITING

"If you don't write when you don't have time for it, you won't write when you do have time for it."

- Katerina Stoykova Klemer

One of the common mistakes aspiring writers make is to not proactively pencil in writing time into their schedule, but keep hoping day after day that somehow they will find the time to write. Naturally, it keeps getting postponed. Writing never gets done that way.

When the deadline strikes, you get into this reactive binge mode and get stressed out to somehow complete your writing project. Instead, why not take a proactive approach to writing by scheduling small chunks of writing time every day ahead of time? First, we need to know how we are spending our time in a given day. May be I am taking too much time to complete a task that ought to take less time. May be I am not the right person to do a particular task and that I have the option of delegating it or outsourcing it or even eliminating it.

So, a simple advice when it comes to finding time to write is this: don't find time to write. You may never be able to find it. Rather make time for writing. Your day is already full and you just have to make time.

All productive writers set aside specific time for writing and they are consistent in following the same routine day after day. We need to take the one big writing goal and split them into projects and specific tasks and schedule them in our daily To-Do lists. If we have "finish the novel" as one of the tasks in the To-Do list, it is never going to be accomplished and will forever remain on the "To-Do" lists causing us untold frustration. This is because it is too overwhelming and too broad of a task to be included in a To-Do list.

What we include in our To-Do list are items that are specific and time-bound. In beginning any writing project, especially the ones that appear to be challenging and vague at the outset, use the concept of SMART goals (more details with an application example can be found in my book, *The Productive Academic Writer*) to break it into:

- **S**pecific: Specific goals help you to focus on narrow and concrete tasks that together make up your writing product at the end.

- **M**easurable: Your specific goal should have a measurable outcome as well as metrics that help you assess your progress towards the goal.

- **A**ttainable: Make your specific and measurable goals achievable by realistically taking into consideration other demands on your time and by having a plan.

- **R**elevant: Is what you are researching/reading or writing relevant to your goal?

- **T**ime-bound: Specific, measurable, attainable, and relevant goals that don't have deadlines are never completed.

One of the ways to schedule your writing for everyday is to do a what-to-expect-for-the-week-ahead review on Saturday or Sunday and create a To-Do list for every day in the week that includes writing as the top priority. Your writing session is scheduled ahead of time right in the beginning of the week. This will also help you to time your writing and understand how much time each writing task takes realistically.

If you feel that your time is passing by just like that, it is time to start tracking how you spend your time. You could either use a pen and paper or use a software app like RescueTime. Always understand that time is a finite resource and no matter how much of an expert you become at time management, there will always be unfinished tasks and more added to your To-Do list constantly. So, we need to just really focus on getting those things done that really matter to us, that are really meaningful and that really bring in 80% of our results.

Here are some interesting facts about prolific writers who used small pockets of time to achieve big results:

- It is said that the French chancellor D'Aguesseau noted that his wife was always 10 minutes late for dinner. So, he decided to use that time for writing his book. Sounds like a very short time to do any serious writing, right? But, writing this way over an year's time (10 minutes x 365 days = 3650 minutes or 60 hours), he published a three-volume book in 1668 that became a best-seller.

- Consider Anthony Trollope who lived between 1815 and 1882. He spent most of his time working as a postal clerk. But, every day he would wake up at 5'o clock and wrote three thousand words in three hours before starting his work. By working like this, he was able to complete 50 books.

- The British novelist, Michael Gilbert was able to get 23 books written during his daily commute of 50 minutes to his daytime job.

APPLICATION EXERCISES

1. If you really feel that you don't have time to write, keep a record of 15-min or 30-min segments of your typical day. Especially note down the time-

wasters – watching TV, browsing the internet with no purpose, etc. How much progress will you be making with your writing if that time could be used for writing?

_____

_____

_____

_____

_____

2. Just for fun, set your alarm clock (if you use one to wake up) or any other device to wake you up one hour before your scheduled rising time. Use that time for writing your book. How much did you get done?

_____

_____

_____

_____

_____

_____

3. Apply the concept of setting SMART writing goals to your writing project by breaking down your project's goal into small, specific, measurable, attainable, relevant, and time-bound goals.

_____

_____

DEVELOP YOUR WRITING ROUTINE

"We are what we repeatedly do. Excellence, then, is not an act, but a habit."

- Aristotle

In describing the work habits of over 161 successful writers, artists, and scientists, Mason Currey notes in his book, *Daily Rituals: How Artists Work?*, how they all went through some sort of self-imposed rituals to get done the work they want to do. For instance, a majority of the writers he profiled in his book got to their work within a couple of hours of rising. Some wrote while standing, some can't get started until they cleaned up the desk, some will only use sharp Number 2 pencils to write, etc. They had a fixed goal and they worked towards reaching that goal day after day (whether it is writing 2,000 words per day or writing for certain number of hours in a day). In other words, they had established routines to achieve their daily productivity goals.

Oftentimes a writer would have to experiment different approaches. The same ritual may not work for everyone. For someone, it may be just forcing oneself to write for 5 minutes. For someone else, that may not work, but they may need a quiet space to get jump started. Basically, the bottom line is that you do the work no matter how you feel and you follow a ritual or a routine because they help you to get into a mindset that is conducive for writing.

For instance, someone may get up, wash their face, and drink a glass of cold water. That is a preparation they do to get into the writing mindset. Think of it as a warm-up you do before starting your daily work-out routine. Of course, a ritual or preparation you do to enter into a writer's mindset is alone not enough to make you write. A writer is someone who is writing!

The single most useful writing advice offered by almost all productive writers and writing coaches is this: write daily in small chunks of time! This is at the heart of developing the writing habit.

First, let us consider the benefits of doing our writing in the morning. That's when our mind is fresh and clear after a good night's sleep and that's the time our creative juices are flowing. And when you get your writing done in the morning and strike it off of your To-Do list, you gain confidence that carries you through the rest of the day. More importantly, it reinforces your desire to achieve your writing goals. There is also a large body of research that shows that creative part of our brain is most active during sleep and right after sleep. On the other hand, the analytical part of our brain (which we want to harness for editing and proofreading tasks) is most active as the day goes by.

Now, someone may say, "Well, guess what? I'm not a morning person, but more of an evening person and that's when my efficiency is high and that's when I get things get done". That's certainly possible.

It is also possible that some may have chronic ailments that do not allow them to function efficiently in the morning or that they find it impossible to include even 30 minutes of writing into their daily morning schedule. Not a big deal. In that case, it is highly suggested that we write at a specific time every day so that we get into a consistent writing routine.

For instance, it is said that Charles Dickens would write in the morning and complete all his writing by 2 p.m. whereas Robert Frost would start his writing sometime around 2 p.m. and write throughout the night. But, they had one thing in common when it came to their writing schedule. They achieved productivity by following the same writing routine day after day.

Cognitive scientists agree that our neural connections are strengthened and reinforced by anything we do consistently as a routine or a habit. So, following a daily writing regimen is good irrespective of whether you are a morning lark, night owl, or a daytime hummingbird.

In the beginning, it helps to monitor your daily output to track your writing progress. All control systems and best management practices include a feedback loop to identify anomalies and to improve the system performance.

The amount of writing you do per day (word count or number of pages) and for what duration is very much quantifiable and something that helps you to identify patterns, the things that you did before and after which impacted your writing goal for the day, how close or far you are with respect to completing your writing project at this rate and so on.

In other words, monitoring your writing output on a weekly basis helps you to identify and reinforce healthy writing habits and avoid habits that lead to reduced writing productivity.

APPLICATION EXERCISES

1. List some time-related and environmental factors that seem to reduce anxiety and favorably influence your writing productivity (ex., "I am most productive when I sit and write first thing in the morning", "I like to do some meditation before getting into writing").

    _____

    _____

    _____

_____

_____

2. Write down one useful lesson you learnt from this chapter.

_____

_____

_____

_____

_____

3. Prepare a chart of your daily writing productivity (time per day or words per day) over a month's period and see if you observe any patterns. Can you explain the highs and the lows?

_____

_____

_____

_____

_____

CHOOSE A CONDUCIVE ENVIRONMENT TO WRITE

> *"Concentrate all your thoughts upon the work at hand. The sun's rays do not burn until brought to a focus."*

- Alexander Graham Bell

Although seasoned writers may be able to get into the flow, irrespective of where they write, choosing a conducive writing environment seems to be critical for those of us who are still developing the writing muscles.

You choose an environment where you feel inspired to write. If you don't like the loneliness of sitting in front of your computer all alone to do your writing, you may want to go to a library or a book store where the mild background noise serves to improve your concentration. Just the sight of books stacked on shelves all around us can increase our motivation to write. Some studies have shown that white noise in the background helps to improve focus as opposed to no noise.

If you feel bored to write, playing some music in the background may move your heart to write. This could either be part of your writing ritual to warm yourself up before writing or the music could go on in the background while you write. Obviously, playing the music loud or playing a song with your favorite lyrics could turn out to be a distraction. So, you may want to choose some music that just sets the mood in the background. Instrumental or classical music may be good choices because they don't contain lyrics and have a soothing effect. If you are getting distracted by the music, don't play it.

Your inspiration for writing can come in a number of ways. Add variety to your life and be open to inspiration. For instance, while cooking one may feel inspired to try a totally new recipe. When you accommodate, invite and are open to inspiration in your other aspects of life, you'll find that inspiration flows more easily in your writing as well. After all, our consciousness is a continuum.

How to Deal with Distractions?

Let us say you want to work on a paper or write a blog. You open the browser to refer to something. One ad/image on the side draws you to go for your favorite online game. After an hour, you are still playing it. You feel guilty and somewhat stressful – yet you can't do anything about it. There is some relation between being connected to the Internet and getting distracted. Is it not ironic that computers, which have been portrayed as a technology that is supposed to enhance our productivity is actually working against us?

The best way to deal with online nuisance is to simply unplug the Ethernet cable or to turn off the Wi-Fi before you start to write. If you are not comfortable with that, there are a number of apps that can temporarily block out your access to certain web sites that you specify: SelfControl for Mac Users, Leecblock (an add-on for Firefox users), Nanny for Google Chrome (as add-on for Chrome users), etc.

Set specific times for "getting distracted" rather than allow distractions to arbitrarily take over you during your scheduled writing session. For instance, if you are habituated to check your e-mails frequently, allocate fixed time for that so that the mind is peaceful and focused while writing.

What about the internal distractions?

Rambling, disoriented thoughts can distract us from focusing on any one objective. It can take us swiftly from one thought to another, and from one continent to another in less than a moment's notice. Unless the mind is peaceful and focused, it is very difficult to focus on writing.

There could be a number of reasons why our mind may be unsettled when we sit down to write, including anxiety, stress, lack of adequate sleep, improper diet, etc. Whatever the reason may be, the result is that an unfocussed mind severely hampers our writing productivity.

There is a growing body of evidence that suggests that daily practice of mindfulness meditation (even as little as 10 minutes per day) can actually help improve our focus and concentration. It can be as simple as *consciously* taking few deep breaths every hour or so at your desk. This slows down your racing thoughts and brings back the focus to the present moment – *the now*. Research has also demonstrated that prayers can help prevent cognitive depletion.

Needless to say that a clean, well-lit, and organized writing space helps you to remain calm and focused. More importantly, it reinforces your desire to achieve your writing goals.

APPLICATION EXERCISES

1. If you are unclear about the sources and instances of typical interruptions during your writing, it is helpful to track them down. How often are you interrupted? What are your most common sources of interruptions? Every time you are interrupted by a phone call or e-mail, jot it down on paper and see how often you are interrupted.

_____

_____

_____

_____

_____

2. Write down one useful lesson you have learnt from this chapter.

_____

_____

_____

_____

_____

3. What are some common sources of stress in your life that may be impacting your writing productivity? How do you plan to deal with it?

_____

_____

_____

_____

_____

⌘

PART V: Get Your Writing Done

⌘

START VERY SMALL AND BUILD ON IT

"A journey of a thousand miles must begin with a single step."

- Lao-Tzu

If you try to make a giant leap forward right at the outset to beat writing procrastination, chances are that you may not be able to keep up your commitment on a daily basis. It is also possible that you may not get started at all because of the perceived pain and boredom associated with your big commitment.

So, start very, very small.

For instance, writing 1,000 or 2,000 words a day can be very intimidating if you have not being doing it for some time. So, rather than setting a tall goal, which can vary from person to person, start with an exceedingly small goal and slowly build it as you become more comfortable and familiar with it.

Just the thought of a particular exercise like weight lifting or some routine may appear intimidating to some. But, by committing oneself to do that exercise or even show up for that exercise for 5 minutes, you have made a big leap forward in addressing that task face to face rather than avoiding it by clever excuses or by postponing it.

This technique could be used to start a new habit or even with established routines and habits which have perceived pain associated with them. We may have completed them so many times, but we do feel the resistance when we have to do it one more time today because of the perceived pain associated with it. So, by starting small, by promising to do it for just 5 minutes, your mental resistance is significantly weakened.

Often we'll find that once we get going, we get going because we figure out that it is not that boring after all.

Take A Writing Challenge or Retreat

"If you wish to be a writer, write."

- Epictetus

By taking a writing challenge, you are committing yourself to writing for a certain period of time (typically 4-5 hours) every day and you are not going to break it anytime during the duration of the challenge. It is the kind of a regimen that you commit yourself to in sticking to an exercise routine or even taking health supplements. You are going to stick to the same time every day. It helps you to form a strong writing habit and brings in a sense of fulfilment and reinforces the desire to write every day.

Take a 14-day, 21-day or 30-day writing challenge. They say that it takes about 21 days to develop a new habit (they must be referring to a positive habit, because bad habits latch on to you faster).

A writing retreat doesn't necessarily mean traveling to meet with a large congregation of writers to get motivated. Certain logistics may prevent that. It may just be you in your study room.

Of course, nowadays, writing retreat is also possible in a virtual setting where writers connect with each other online and commit to a rigid writing schedule. It definitely helps to work with like-minded individuals for mutual support and accountability to develop the habit of daily writing.

Use If-Then Planning

"Plans are nothing; planning is everything."

- Dwight D. Eisenhower

One of the ways procrastination manifests is in the form of "I'll do it someday". In other words, you know very well that a task needs to be accomplished, but because you have not defined to yourself when you will accomplish it, it gets postponed forever and ever. Something that may take just 5 minutes gets postponed for 5 years just because I have not planned for when I will get it completed.

In terms of writing, this tip is very similar to the idea of pro-actively scheduling your daily writing time, but it goes one step further to completely eliminate procrastination by putting a time next to when you will get a certain aspect of your writing accomplished. We all know that writing is not just the writing part, but it includes editing, formatting, etc. Research has shown that those who use "If-then" planning are far more likely to get things done than those who don't. Here is where I came across this idea: Implementation Intentions.

If-then planning is effective because you commit to do a specific activity at your assigned time. The way it works is that you write down, "if X happens, do Y". For instance, "if it is 8 a.m. in the morning, write for 30 minutes". It is a powerful way to build a habit as well as to reinforce a habit. You could extend this by adding any anticipated scenario that may prevent you from completing this task. For instance, "if it is 8 a.m., and if I feel bored to write, I will do jumping jacks for a few minutes". As you can see there is no room for negotiation here because you have clearly spelled out what you'll do when you are faced with potential obstacles to accomplish your writing task.

If you are still finding yourself regularly postponing (read procrastinating) your writing, you may want to use some sort of a 'pre-commitment' device where you set something at stake. For instance, writers use the 'write-or-die' software to get into the habit of speed writing because the consequences of not reaching your writing goal (e.x., 500 words in a hour) can range anywhere from having to hear an annoying sound to your words disappearing one after another on the monitor.

CREATE A SENSE OF URGENCY

"Time and tide waits for none."

- Geoffrey Chaucer

When you set a deadline for your book writing project, you create a sense of urgency. Here you are focused on getting your writing done by the deadline you have set. We may set a deadline, but conveniently forget about it either intentionally or as we get busy in the hustle-bustle of life.

Writing it on a sticky-note and having it posted it at the corner of your monitor or on your writing desk will serve as a constant reminder that you cannot ignore. Some authors find it efficient to sign a contract to themselves promising that they are going to finish their book on such and such a date. Some authors do a pre-release because they know that they need to complete their book by the pre-assigned release date.

First, have a goal.

Second, you determine how many pages you want to write and break that into small chunks of time/pages that spread over a specified duration (two weeks or three weeks). Then have a target for each day (i.e., complete 1000 words) and work towards it without fail.

Creating a sense of urgency is very important to get a task accomplished. John P. Kotter, the author of *A Sense of Urgency* provides some key tactics for increasing urgency and rooting out complacency (without mistaking activity for productivity). Unless we set a deadline, we will keep postponing the task. The famous Parkinson's Law states that "work contracts to fit in the time we give it." So, if you have a deadline to submit your article in two weeks, you'll most likely complete it in 14 days. That's how it works. Don't we experience that every year when it is time to file taxes? So, why not create a sense of urgency by assigning a deadline to every writing task we perform? In effect we go from one time-bound task to another throughout the day and throughout our life. When we start tracking our time like this, we may be surprised to learn how much time we waste.

Setting a deadline not only applies to our writing project but also to everything we do. And when we do become comfortable and efficient working with self-imposed deadlines, we can challenge ourselves to completing a task earlier than the time we have assigned it.

On a daily basis, you can create a sense of urgency by setting a timer every time you write. There are many stopwatch and timer apps and software available both for online and offline use. For Windows, the following FREE timer applications seem to be popular owing to their simplicity: Orzeszek Timer, Focus Booster, and CookTimer. For Mac users, the Timer for Mac application is the most popular.

Unless you have already established consistent and steady levels of daily writing output, it is a good idea to stop writing when the timer goes off. This will ensure that you don't get into the euphoric binge-writing mode on days you feel super-excited about writing which can't be sustained even the very next day.

First, establish a regulated daily writing routine (30 minutes a day is good to begin with) and then gradually increase it as you go along, if needed. Don't forget to give yourself a treat. It can be as simple as taking a walk; however it should be something you enjoy as it positively reinforces your writing habit.

Developing the healthy habit of writing in small chunks of time daily goes a long way in achieving the goal of steady and sustained productivity. One useful technique to implement this practice is the Pomodoro Technique. Pomodoro is an Italian word that means tomato. The Pomodoro Technique, named after the tomato-shaped kitchen timer that Cirillo first used as a University student, is based on the fact that small periods of focused effort with no distractions and lots of breaks improve the mental agility and help us become more productive in writing rather than adopting a bite-all-at-once approach.

In the Pomodoro Technique, you break down the time it will take for a massive task to be accomplished into small time intervals (typically 25 minutes in length) followed by short breaks. After four pomodori (plural for pomodoro), you get the reward of a longer break, anywhere from 15-30 minutes.

Multi-tasking is not going to help with your writing. Contrary to the opinion that we can be more productive by doing multi-tasking, studies have shown that only 2% of people can multi-task and the remaining 98% get distracted and become under-productive by multi-tasking. So, it is better to just focus on task at hand using time-blocking systems like Pomodoro Technique, than get stressed out by trying multi-task while writing.

BE ACCOUNTABLE

"Accountability breeds response-ability."

- Stephen R. Covey

It is a well-known fact that humans tend to align their behavior depending on how accountable they are. Psychologists have studied this phenomenon and have coined the term *Hawthorne effect*: one is careful with one's actions when one is being observed than when one is not.

For instance, for an academic (something I am more familiar with), there is a lack of built-in accountability when it comes to writing. Somehow, teaching, service and other position responsibilities get accomplished because there is some inherent accountability built into those responsibilities. For instance, if you don't teach well, you get immediate feedback from students. But, when it comes to writing there is no accountability. You can postpone it, avoid it, resist it and nothing happens until you get to a stage where you realize that you can't get your tenure or that you get fired.

So, when you are aware that you are being monitored, you are more likely to follow through on your commitments. This is a great tool to fight against procrastination in writing.

Nowadays, there a number of ways to make yourself publicly accountable through apps, by joining live or online groups where you can connect with like-minded people and get feedback and support. Although the thought of this may make you nervous, it has the benefit of making you more accountable and giving you the needed push to get your writing done.

For writers, there are a number of online writing groups. You can either have a buddy or a partner to whom you can make yourself accountable to in terms of the progress you are making and how you are meeting the deadlines.

Apart from the primary benefit of helping you to become more accountable, joining a writing group offers you the opportunity to connect with other writers functioning in a similar environment as you. It can help you overcome feelings of frustration, isolation and shame that can often come in the way of productive writing.

REWARD YOURSELF REGULARLY

*"Don't judge each day by the harvest you reap,
but by the seeds that you plant."*

- Robert Louis Stevenson

Tasks that are most likely to be procrastinated include those that one is averse to, those which come with distant rewards, and those that are boring. Since writing is considered a long-haul process associated with a distant reward (if any), we like to postpone it by replacing it with a task that produces instant gratification.

So, by minimizing the perceived pain associated with writing and by maximizing the pleasure associated with doing it, the chances are higher that it actually gets done.

In other words, have some kind of a reward to motivate yourself to get your writing done. There is certainly some cheating involved in doing this, but it is

OK to use it to cheat ourselves out of procrastination. Because, by procrastination we are cheating ourselves big time.

We are already somewhat familiar with this idea of reinforcing non-preferred behaviors (that which we are averse to) with preferred behaviors (what which we like to do), which is known as the Premack Principle in the field of psychology. For instance, when we didn't want to do our homework, our parents told us that we get to go out and play for some time if we completed the homework. We happily complied and even got the homework done sooner to get to the thing that was of real interest to us. Similarly, when we were sick and we had to be given some bitter medicine, it was mixed with applesauce or something sweet. It was a win-win for us as well as our parents because their goal (medicine) was achieved and we got the applesauce.

So, until we find writing itself to be the reward, we do need some kind of reward to keep ourselves motivated and encouraged. The reward we choose doesn't have to be something extraordinary. We could identify some of the fun activities we already like doing and turn them into rewards. For instance, if you enjoy going out on a walk in the woods, something you'll definitely do no matter what, then make a commitment that you'll reward yourself with a walk in the woods after you complete your scheduled writing session for a fixed amount of time.

Assign smaller rewards for accomplishing smaller goals and larger rewards for accomplishing major goals. Over time, you will not need any external reward for getting your writing done, but writing itself becomes your reward. When that happens, you will get your writing done whether you find it pleasurable or painful.

A final note.

Productivity is all about balance and making enthusiastic, but detached efforts. It is not about endeavoring too much to achieve one goal at the cost of sacrificing others. If you are absorbed in the thoughts of planning your next book while you spend your time with your loved ones, it is going to take a toll on your personal relationships sooner or later. On the other hand, by living a balanced life that includes physical, intellectual, emotional, and social developmental activities, you will avoid the pitfall of a burnout that comes with taking a one-sided approach to improve your writing productivity.

Lessons Learned

RECAP

"As to methods there may be a million and then some, but principles are few. One who grasps principles can successfully select their own methods. One who tries methods, ignoring principles, is sure to have trouble."

- Ralph Waldo Emerson

PART I: Plan your writing

Identify your purpose

- What is your purpose behind writing a book? Writing is a long-haul process and although you may start off the project with great enthusiasm and energy, what will really help you to not run out of steam is to have a grounded purpose and to keep revisiting this purpose again and again.

Consider your target audience

- Professional writers always write to delight their target audience. Keeping your audience in mind while writing your book helps you to: more easily decide what materials to include and what not to include in your writing; decide on your writing style; decide on how much to explain; organize your ideas and consider different approaches to writing.

Examine your writing situation

- A writing plan helps you to plan for any expected or unexpected obstacles on the way and helps you to achieve steady levels of productivity. How much time can you realistically put in every day towards your book writing project? The more complex your life is, the more detailed your writing plan needs to be.

- This is also the time to address your initial anxieties or fears about writing. It is important to recognize that most of these anxieties and fears you may be experiencing are situational and not long-standing or pervasive in your writing life.

- Here are some key strategies for overcoming your initial anxieties about writing:

  o Choose a writing partner or a writing buddy from whom you can get support, encouragement and feedback;

o If you are more of a speaker than writer, you may find yourself more comfortable speaking your book or portions of your book and then transcribing it to get your first draft;

o If you find that your chosen topic is too broad or has multiple audiences, consider bringing them out in the form of a series of short books;

o Cultivate a habit of rewarding yourself with simple successes in your writing life such as getting started, drafting the outline, etc.

PART II: Gather ideas and create your outline

Start with yourself

▪ First, start with yourself as the source before even looking up what others have written on that particular topic. Before directly plunging into researching about your topic or doing a literature review, draw on your own experiences and your prior knowledge of that topic.

Keep an idea book

▪ Good writers are always curious and continually developing themselves, learning the world around them. So, always carry with you an idea book or flash cards to jot down what you see, what you experience. Ideas can come anytime and can also vanish like snowflakes anytime.

Maintain a journal

- Your journal is your personal space for developing ideas and thoughts as you interact with the world around you. Amazingly, many times you'll find that in that free flow of thoughts, you'll find hidden gems which are new ideas for your writing projects.

Do freewriting

- Don't start your writing session with a blank screen, but always approach it with a plan of what it is that you'll be writing about during that session. If you don't have a plan, do some freewriting and get the writing gears moving.

- To get started, write down whatever comes to your mind (brain-dump) without worrying about the quality or nature of the content. After a few initial freewriting sessions, practice focused freewriting on a specific topic for a specified duration.

Hold brainstorming writing sessions

- Brainstorming is a process to generate as many ideas as possible relating to a specific topic or interest. It maximizes the ability to generate ideas by suspending judgment and by separating the idea creation process and the evaluation process.

- While brainstorming, if you feel that you are running out of ideas, here are some ways you can use to stimulate your thinking: cubing, similes, use journalists' questions (who, what, when, why, where, and how), map your ideas.

Create your outline

- After completing one or more of brainstorming writing sessions, you will have either a list of keywords or phrases or even better a map, from which you can develop your book outline.

- Having some kind of an outline, even a rough one, is like having driving directions when you want to get from place A to place B. Once you have an outline, it is much easier to focus on one sub-section at a time and start building your writing project.

PART III: Develop your content: from first draft to finished book

Write your book bit by bit

- Take one specific topic at a time and focus on building content. You could do this through one or more scheduled writing sessions devoted to each topic.

- If you are finding it hard to get started, use one or more brainstorming writing sessions (which you are already familiar with) on each of your book's topic to identify things that should be covered. Especially, use the journalist questions (Who, What, When, Why, Where, How) to think from your reader's perspective and to raise relevant questions and answer them.

- As you do research and/or review published and unpublished sources to gather information to assist in your writing, use the journalists' questions as lenses to look for information that you need. Otherwise, the whole process of researching and reviewing literature can be overwhelming and exceedingly time consuming with very little output.

- If you are unable to move forward with one topic after a certain point, move to another topic. You don't have to write linearly and sequentially if that is not working out for you. You can always reorganize your topics and make connections between different chapters later.

- Hold several freewriting sessions to get your messy first draft. Don't edit as you write, but save it for the future. Similarly, do not look up words or do research while you write. If there is really a need, make a note of it as you write and get back to it later.

Speak your book

- If you find it more comfortable to speak about one or more topics in your book than to sit down and write it, then use it to your advantage. In essence, this method lets you first create your audiobook or portions of it and then transcribe it to get the content for your digital or print version. Identify a topic, prepare a list of questions, interview yourself and record your answers, and get it transcribed to get your first draft.

- One big advantage to transcribing the audio yourself is that you get to hear yourself speak about your book. This boosts your confidence as a writer and brings in focus and concentration that enables you to consider additional perspectives on your topic not covered in your talk.

Rewrite, revise, and edit your book

- Irrespective of whether you write your book bit by bit or speak your book, what you have in your hand is only a first draft, and not the final draft. You still need to rewrite it, revise it, and edit it.

- Set a deadline for your editing task. Otherwise, your editing will never get done.

PART IV: Systematize your writing process

Identify your writing challenges

- External challenges are those that are beyond our control. Internal challenges manifest in the form of resistance to writing in subtle, clever ways. For instance, you determine yourself to write and you are all set to write. But, then suddenly you are overtaken by the urge to do something else and you end up doing that instead of writing. Take two minutes to identify what throws you off right at that moment you start to write.

Overcome perfectionism and negative self-talk

- When we set a very high standard for what our writing should come out to be, we are setting ourselves up for frustration and failure because there is not a single piece of work that has been agreed upon by everyone.

- We need to understand that the healthy pursuit of excellence is helpful and energizing while the striving for artificial standards of perfection is unhealthy and disempowering.

- Here are some practical tips to overcome perfectionistic tendencies in writing:

  o Don't think of your writing as the next earth-shattering masterpiece. Rather, consider it as a "rough first draft", "write-up", etc. and refer to it as such;

  o Accept that "to err is human" and that we all mistakes. No matter how hard we may try, we will still make mistakes;

  o Set your productivity goals (can even be a simple commitment as writing 5 minutes a day) after realistically taking into your consideration other priorities and commitments;

- o Don't judge your output by how great you felt or how bad you felt while writing. In other words, don't judge your output at all;

- o By all means, seek social and professional support, feedback and guidance.

- Another major obstacle to free-flowing writing is the defeatist mindset that can range anywhere from indulging in negative self-talk with our mind and with others who espouse a similar approach to developing a deep aversion to writing by repeatedly labeling ourselves with negative adjectives. Practice of breathing exercise, mindful writing, and replacing negative thoughts with positive, hope-giving thoughts can help you to silence your inner critic.

Make time for writing

- A simple advice when it comes to finding time to write is this: don't find time to write. You may never be able to find it. Rather make time for writing.

- All productive writers set aside specific time for writing and they are consistent in following the same routine day after day.

- In beginning any writing project, especially the ones that appear to be challenging and vague at the outset, use the concept of SMART writing goals to break it into: narrow, specific, measurable, attainable, relevant, and time-bound tasks.

- One of the ways to schedule your writing for everyday is to do a what-to-expect-for-the-week-ahead review on Saturday or Sunday and create a To-Do list for every day in the week that includes writing as the top priority. Your writing session is scheduled ahead of time right in the beginning of the week. This will also help you to time your writing and understand how much time each writing task takes realistically.

Develop your writing routine

- Many successful artists and writers use self-imposed rituals to get around obstacles and get done the work they enjoy to do. They had established routines to achieve their daily productivity goals. Such rituals and routines seem to reduce the feelings of anxiety and insecurity associated with writing and help one enter into a writer's mindset.

- The single most useful writing advice offered by almost all productive writers and writing coaches is this: write daily in small chunks of time! This is at the heart of developing the writing habit.

- If possible, the best time to get your writing done is in the morning when the mind is fresh, creative juices are flowing, and your will power reserve is supposed be at its peak.

- Our neural connections are strengthened and reinforced by anything we do consistently as a routine or a habit. So, following a daily writing regimen is good irrespective of whether you are a morning lark, night owl, or a daytime hummingbird.

- It helps to monitor your daily output to track your writing progress. Monitoring your writing output on a weekly basis helps you to identify and reinforce healthy writing habits and avoid habits that lead to reduced writing productivity.

Choose a conducive environment to write

- You choose an environment where you feel inspired to write. If you feel bored to write, playing some music in the background may move your heart to write.

- The best way to deal with online nuisance is to simply unplug the Ethernet cable or to turn off the Wi-Fi before you start to write. If you are not comfortable with that, use one of the freely available apps to temporarily block out your access to certain web sites that you specify.

- Set specific times for "getting distracted" rather than allow distractions to arbitrarily take over you during your scheduled writing session. For instance, if you are habituated to check your e-mails frequently, allocate fixed time for that so that the mind is peaceful and focused while writing.

- Rambling, disoriented thoughts can distract us from focusing on any one objective. As simple as *consciously* taking few deep breaths every hour or so at your writing desk can slow down your racing thoughts and brings back the focus to the present moment – *the now.*

PART V: Get your writing done

Start very small and build on it

- We often procrastinate writing because of the perceived pain and boredom associated with the commitment and discipline that goes with writing. If you set a high writing goal (such as writing 1,000 words a day) for yourself right in the beginning, chances are that you may not get started at all or not be able to keep up your commitment on a daily basis. So, start exceedingly small and build on it gradually.

Take a writing challenge or retreat

- Take a 14-day, 21-day or 30-day writing challenge where you get together (in physical or virtual space) with other individuals in similar situations to commit yourself to write for a fixed period of time throughout the duration of challenge. They say that it takes about 21 days to develop a new habit (they must be referring to a positive habit, because bad habits latch on to you faster).

Use If-Then planning

- One of the ways procrastination manifests is in the form of "I'll do it someday". In other words, you know very well that a task needs to be accomplished, but because you have not defined to yourself when you will accomplish it, it gets postponed forever and ever. If-then planning is effective because you commit to do a specific activity at your assigned time. For instance, "if it is 8 AM in the morning, write for 30 minutes".

Create a sense of urgency

- When you set a deadline for your book writing project, you create a sense of urgency. First, have a goal. Second, you determine how many pages you want to write and break that into small chunks of time/pages that spread over a specified duration (two weeks or three weeks). Then have a target for each day (i.e., complete 1000 words) and work towards it without fail.

- On a daily basis, you can create a sense of urgency by setting a timer every time you write. There are many stopwatch and timer apps and software available both for online and offline use.

- Developing the healthy habit of writing in small chunks of time daily goes a long way in achieving the goal of steady and sustained productivity. Many authors and writers have found the Pomodoro Technique to be useful in this regard. In the Pomodoro Technique, you break down the time it will take for a massive task to be accomplished into small time intervals (typically 25 minutes in length) followed by short breaks. After four pomodori (plural for pomodoro), you get the reward of a longer break, anywhere from 15-30 minutes.

Be accountable

- It is a well-known fact that humans tend to align their behavior depending on how accountable they are. Psychologists have studied this phenomenon and have coined the term, Hawthorne effect: one is careful with one's actions when one is being observed than when one is not.

- Nowadays, there a number of ways to make yourself publicly accountable through apps, by joining live or online groups where you can connect with like-minded people and get feedback and support.

- Apart from the primary benefit of helping you to become more accountable, joining a writing group offers you the opportunity to connect with other writers functioning in a similar environment as you. It can help you overcome feelings of frustration, isolation and shame that can often come in the way of productive writing.

Reward yourself regularly

- Have some kind of a reward to motivate yourself to get your writing done and to reinforce the writing habit. Assign smaller rewards for accomplishing smaller goals and larger rewards for accomplishing major writing goals. Until we find writing itself to be the reward, we do need some kind of reward to keep ourselves motivated and encouraged.

Wish you a happy and productive writing experience!

BIBLIOGRAPHY

Allen, D. Getting Things Done: The Art of Stress-Free Productivity. Rev. ed. New York: Penguin, 2015.

Atchity, K. A Writer's Time: Making the Time to Write. Rev. ed. New York: W. W. Norton, 1995.

Baumeister, R. F. and Tierney, J. Willpower: Rediscovering the Greatest Human Strength. New York: The Penguin Press, 2011.

Brown, B. The Gifts of Imperfection. Let Go of Who You Think You're Supposed to Be and Embrace Who You Are. Center City, Minnesota: Hazelden Publishing, 2010.

Cameron, J. The Artist's Way: A Spiritual Path to Higher Creativity. Rev. ed. New York: Putnam, 2002.

Carson, R. Taming Your Gremlin: A Surprisingly Simple Method for Getting Out of Your Own Way. New York: HarperCollins, 2003.

Covey, S. R. The 7 Habits of Highly Effective People: Powerful Lessons in Personal Change. New York: Free Press, 2004.

Duhigg, C. The Power of Habit: Why We Do What We Do in Life and Business. New York: Random House, 2014.

Elbow, P. Writers Without Teachers. London: Oxford University Press, 1998.

Fiore, N. The Now Habit: A Strategic Program for Overcoming Procrastination and Enjoying Guilt-Free Play. New York: Tarcher/Penguin, 2007.

Fryxell, D. A. Write Faster, Write Better: Time-saving Techniques for Writing Great Fiction and Nonfiction. Cincinnati, OH: Writer's Digest Books, 2004.

Goldberg, N. Writing Down the Bones: Freeing the Writer Within. Rev. ed. Boston: Shambhala, 2005.

Gross, G. Editors on Editing: What Writers Need to Know About What Editors Do. 3rd Rev. ed. New York: Grove/Atlantic, 1993.

Kabat-Zinn, J. Full Catastrophe Living: Using the Wisdom of Your Body and Mind to Face Stress, Pain, and Illness. Rev. ed. New York: Random House, 2013.

Klauser, H. A. Writing on Both Sides of the Brain: Breakthrough Techniques for People Who Write. New York: HarperCollins, 1987.

Klauser, H. A. Write It Down, Make It Happen: Knowing What You Want – And Getting It! New York: Simon and Schuster, 2001.

Lambert, N. M. Publish and Prosper: A Strategy Guide for Students and Researchers. 1st ed. New York: Routledge, 2014.

Lamott, A. Bird by Bird: Some Instructions on Writing and Life. 1st Ed. New York: Anchor Books, 1995.

O'Hanlon, B. Write is A Verb. Sit Down. Start Writing. No Excuses. Cincinnati, OH: Writer's Digest Books, 2007.

Pressfield, S. The War of Art: Break Through the Blocks and Win Your Inner Creative Battles. New York: Black Irish Books, 2002.

Ramage, J. D., Bean, J. C., and Johnson, J. The Allyn & Bacon Guide to Writing. Brief ed. (7th ed.). New Jersey: Pearson, 2014.

Rettig, H. The 7 Secrets of the Prolific: The Definitive Guide to Overcoming Procrastination, Perfectionism, and Writer's Block. Infinite Art, 2011.

Rocquemore, K. A. Shut Up and Write. Inside Higher Ed. June 14, 2010.

Ross-Larson, B. Edit Yourself. New York: W. W. Norton, 1982.

Silvia, P. J. How to Write a Lot: A Practical Guide to Productive Academic Writing. Washington, DC: American Psychological Association, 2007.

Stone, H. and Stone, S. Embracing Your Inner Critic: Turning Self-Criticism into A Creative Asset. San Francisco, CA: HarperCollins, 2011.

Strunk, W. and White, E. B. The Elements of Style. 3rd Ed. New York: Macmillan, 1979.

**An Easy-To-Read Guide to
Low-Stress Prolific Writing**

The Productive
Academic
Writer

Kasthurirangan Gopalakrishnan, Ph.D.

"If you have had the intention to write something, but you have not been able to achieve your goal, *The Productive Academic Writer* will explain why you haven´t and what you can do to make your intentions a reality….I am sure academic writing teachers and writers, in general, really appreciate being understood by another writer, Gopalakrishnan, who had the time to present our doubts and common stressful situations with answers to overcome all of them."

- Prof. Beatriz Manrique, University of Zulia, Maracaibo, Venezuela

"There are plenty books on the market telling the would-be author (academic or otherwise) how to write with clarity and grammatical precision. There are fewer books dealing with the issue of how to get motivated to write in the first place. That's why "The Productive Academic Writer" is so useful, for it provides sound advice, which, if followed, is sure to make the would-be writer more disciplined and productive…Although this book is primarily written for people in academia (where one's job often depends on written productivity), anyone who writes a lot, whether as an avocation or a career, will benefit from its advice."

- Dr. Doug Erlandson (Amazon Top 50 Reviewer), Adjunct Instructor of Philosophy, Southeast Community College, Lincoln, NE

"The Productive Academic Writer is a timely help for me, a novice researcher who always struggles with the task academic writing and feels stressed out by it. The limiting beliefs described in the book, like perfectionism,

procrastination, and lack of accountability, are too familiar to me. Academic writing seems much more a mental, rather than intellectual, obstacle to me! The book presents an assortment of wonderful and practical solutions to my problems with writing. I am really fond of such tips as "free writing", "daily writing", and "the Pomodoro technique", etc., which, I believe, serve to foster importantly healthy writing habits for me and many other like-minded struggling academics. More interestingly, this book provides the links to useful software or apps for us to put those techniques into practice. For academics aspiring to improve their writing productivity, it is an "engaging and easy-to-read" book worth reading and remembering."

- Prof. Weiqiang Wang, School of English for International Business, Guangdong University of Foreign Studies, China

"I will definitely recommend this book to my students and colleagues. It has also helped me a lot to recognize problems that I have with writing. For me, the added value is the concise, yet extremely valuable, exposition of the problems that potential writers face leading to failure in writing, and how to overcome them. Easy-to-read, convince yourself and you're writing."

- Dr. Rogelio Palomera-Garcia, Professor, Department of Electrical & Computer Engineering, University of Puerto Rico at Mayaguez, Puerto Rico

"The Productive Academic Writer: An Easy-To-Read Guide To Low-Stress Prolific Writing is a useful guide which addresses academic writing, an important issue of academics who are affected by a range of factors. In this book, Kasthurirangan Gopalakrishnan asserts that although productive writing is key to success, many people have different idiosyncrasies and blocks which prevent them from being academic writers. This book is very useful for people struggling to find out what affects their writing, and also offers solutions and systematically points out useful books which provide further info in each case... Overall, I found the book useful, with wide appeal, and I felt that it was very down to earth, direct, and sympathetic while denouncing an unduly harsh approach to writing productivity."

- *Reviewed By Nandita Keshavan for Readers' Favorite (5 stars)*

www.ingramcontent.com/pod-product-compliance
Lightning Source LLC
Chambersburg PA
CBHW050134280326
41933CB00010B/1373